Madrid

EDICIONES
Aldeasa

P. 2
Puerta de Alcalá.

P. 4, 5
Calle de Alcalá.

Madrid of yesteryear

THE ORIGINS OF MADRID ARE HUMBLE. THE FIRST RELIABLE HISTORICAL MENTION WE HAVE IS FROM THE LATE 9TH CENTURY, WHEN THE EMIR OF CORDOBA MOHAMMED I BUILT A FORTRESS ON A PROMONTORY NEXT TO THE RIVER MANZANARES. THIS SIMPLE FORTIFICATION FORMED PART OF THE DEFENSIVE NETWORK THAT PROTECTED TOLEDO. AFTER BEING RECONQUERED BY THE CHRISTIANS, THE SMALL SETTLEMENT GRADUALLY GAINED IMPORTANCE UNTIL ESTABLISHING ITSELF AS A CASTILIAN VILLA OR TOWN. THE DETERMINANT EVENT THAT CHANGED THE DESTINY OF THE CITY FOREVER TOOK PLACE IN JUNE 1561, WHEN PHILLIP II ORDERED THE COURT TO BE MOVED TO MADRID. THIS DECISION SUDDENLY TURNED THE TOWN INTO THE CENTRE OF HIS EMPIRE AND CHANGED ITS HISTORY AND APPEARANCE FOREVER.

THE LABYRINTH OF NARROW STREETS AND SQUARES THAT EXTEND FROM CALLE BAILÉN AS FAR AS PASEO DEL PRADO, FORM THE MAIN PART OF THE HISTORICAL AND MONUMENTAL LEGACY OF THE CITY. HERE ARE CONCENTRATED MANY OF THE MOST BEAUTIFUL AND EMBLEMATIC SPOTS, AS WELL AS SOME OF THE MOST CHARMING CORNERS. STROLLING AROUND THIS INTRICATELY LAID OUT AREA IN WHICH BUILDINGS, PALACES, CHURCHES AND CONVENTS OF DIVERSE STYLES AND PERIODS APPEAR BEFORE US IN NO APPARENT ORDER, ONE CAN SEE THE EVOLUTION OF THE CITY SINCE ITS FOUNDING UNTIL THE PRESENT. ITS BUSY STREETS FULL OF FLAVOUR ARE STILL THE HEART OF THE NEW CONTEMPORARY CITY CENTRE. WALKING AROUND THEM IS ENTERING INTO A CHAOTIC AND DELICIOUS SHOW, IN WHICH THE HISTORY OF THE CITY IS IRREMEDIABLY MIXED WITH ITS MOST PALPITATING AND MODERN SIDE. THE IDEAL PLACE TO CHECK OUT MADRID AND ITS PEOPLE.

Cathedral of the Almudena.

P. 8-10

The Plaza de Oriente is one of the essential settings of the old Madrid and one of the most beautiful and important of the whole city. It is overlooked by the magnificent building of the Palacio Real, which continues being the official residence of the Spanish Royal Family, although today it is only used for diverse ceremonies and official acts. This splendid square was created during the reign of Joseph Bonaparte I with the aim of creating a large and suitable setting for the palace and its environs.

P. 11

Opposite the palace is the Teatro Real, which is the city opera house. It was opened in 1850 and, after an eventful history, was heavily reformed between 1991 and 1997. Today, due to its acoustics and technical conditions, it is one of the best venues for performing opera in Europe.

The Palacio Real is situated on a hill alongside the River Manzanares, in an area that has been closely linked to the history of the city since its origins. Phillip V was the monarch who ordered the construction of this magnificent building after a fire had almost completely destroyed the old Royal Palace on Christmas Eve of 1734. The works were carried out between 1738 and 1755 under the direction of the Italian architect Juan Bautista Sachetti, who had the cooperation of, among others, Ventura Rodríguez and Sabatini. The lovely gardens surrounding the palace are from later periods. The Sabatini Gardens (photo), in the northern part, were built in the thirties and are of French design, while what is called Campo del Moro was rebuilt after years of abandon during the reign of María Cristina, following the model of 19th-century English parks.

P. 14, 15

The Plaza de la Villa, situated in the very heart of Hapsburg Madrid, is without doubt one of the most beautiful and best-conserved spots of old Madrid. It is a quiet and attractive pedestrian-only area. Visiting it and strolling around the narrow adjoining streets is a delightful way of coming close to the history of the city. Within the small perimeter of the square there are three buildings of great value. Casa de la Villa, currently the City Old council, began to be built in 1644 following a project by Juan Gómez de Mora. Right beside it is the impressive Casa de Cisneros, an ele-gant palace in Plateresque style. The oldest property in the square is Casa de los Lujanes, built throughout the 15th century as a stately home for this powerful dynasty. The lovely masonry and brick tower is the most interest-ing part of the series of buildings.

P. 16–19

The Plaza Mayor has been, since construction began on it in the late-16th century, one of the city's major public spaces. This exceptional arcaded area was the first monumental square to be built in Madrid and is still today one of the city's epicentres. It is a spot of exceptional beauty crossed by thousands of local Madrid people and visitors every day. The current appearance of the square dates from 1790, when after a terrible destructive fire its reconstruction was undertaken by Juan de Villanueva. Throughout its long history, the Plaza Mayor has been the setting for all kinds of events: royal festivals, bullfights, markets, auto-da-fes and even public executions. Today, both the square and the adjoining streets are still brimming with life and flavour.

P. 20

The Puerta del Sol is the indispensable reference point and busy centre of the city. The construction of the Real Casa de Correos in 1768, currently the offices of the Presidency of the Community of Madrid, began to outline the urban layout of this well-known Madrid square. In the last 150 years the Puerta del Sol has been witness to some of the events that have shaped the recent history of Spain. It was the setting of such important events as the Esquilache mutiny, the popular uprising against the Napoleonic troops, the repatriation of Ferdinand VI or the proclamation of the Second Republic.

P. 21

In recent years, a great effort has been made to rehabilitate historical buildings in the central area. A magnificent example has been the recent remodelling of the Posada del Peine, which was opened around 1610 and is thought to be the oldest hotel in Madrid.

P. 22

Two monumental bronze chariots crown the building of the Banco de Bilbao, work of the architect Ricardo Bastida y Bilbao. In this first section of Calle de Alcalá you can take in several magnificently-constructed buildings that were erected as head offices of diverse financial entities during the first decades of the last century.

P. 23

The Metrópolis building, with its spectacular dome with scales, crowned by a winged Victory, occupies the intersection between the two most emblematic avenues of the city centre, Gran Vía and Calle de Alcalá. It was built between 1905 and 1911 by the French architects Jules and Raymond Février.

P. 24, 25

One of the great icons of the city is undoubtedly the Fountain of Cibeles that overlooks the square of the same name, one of the most beautiful in Madrid. The fountain was designed by Ventura Rodríguez and opened in 1782. It represents the Goddess Cybele, the goddess of the Earth, agriculture and fertility, on a chariot pulled by two lions. Surrounding this spectacular monument are four magnificent buildings: the imposing headquarters of the Banco de España; the spectacular Palacio de Comunicaciones (New City Council), built by Antonio Palacios and Julián Otamendi; the Palacio de Buenavista, home of the General Headquarters of the Land Army, and the Palacio de Linares, currently Casa de América.

REGE CAROLO III
ANNO
MDCCLXXVIII

P. 26, 27

Charles III has entered the history books as one of the monarchs who did most to embellish and modernise the city. The Puerta de Alcalá, designed by Francisco Sabatini and opened in 1778, is one of the most representative monuments of his reign and one of the most emblematic of the whole city. Curiously, the inscription on the attic of the central section is written in Italian (Sabatini's mother tongue) and not in Latin or Castilian as one would expect.

P. 28, 29

The Puerta de Alcalá stands out for its elegant neoclassical features and balance. The current gateway replaced a previous one and was ordered to be built by Charles III, since he did not like it. With the aim of building a new one a tender was put out with bids from architects of the category of Ventura Rodríguez and José de Hermosilla, the project presented by Sabatini finally being chosen. This spectacular monument is made up of five openings, three of them with semicircular arches and the other two lintelled. The sculptures crowning the keystones and cornice were made by Roberto Michel.

P. 30–34

The beautiful fountain of Neptuno enjoys a privileged position between two of the greatest art galleries in the city, the Prado National Museum and the Thyssen-Bornemisza Museum. It was designed by Ventura Rodríguez and made between 1780 and 1784 by Juan Pascual de Mena. It is made of white marble and represents the God of the Sea, with a trident in one hand and a curled up snake in the other, on a chariot made up of a shell pulled by two seahorses. The sculptural series formed part of the original remodelling project of what was called the Salón del Prado.

P. 35

The famous lions that adorn the doors of the Palacio del Congreso de los Diputados (Spanish Parliament building), in Carrera de San Jerónimo, were made from the bronze of two cannons requisitioned during the War of Africa (1859-1860). The building, in neoclassical style, was built by Narciso Pascual y Colomer in 1850.

P. 36

The monastery of the Descalzas Reales (in the photo) and that of the Encarnación are two beautiful convents situated in the very heart of the old city centre. The two royal monasteries were built in the early 16th century and created a school of design. Both also house excellent works of art.

P. 37

One of the most charming corners of Madrid is the small Plaza de las Comendadoras, very close to the old Cuartel de Conde Duque. This welcoming space is marvellous for evoking the atmosphere and flavour of the Madrid of yesteryear. The terraces facing the square are a wonderful spot to sit down and enjoy the relaxing rhythm of the setting. The convent of the Comendadoras de Santiago, which is built on one of the sides, gives off a real feeling of calm and contemplation. It was built under the direction of Manuel and José del Olmo during the second half of the 17th century.

Madrid today

MADRID SURPRISES THE TRAVELLER DUE TO ITS FRENETIC PACE, ITS CONTAGIOUS VITALITY AND DUE TO ITS PASSIONATE SYMBIOSIS BETWEEN TRADITION AND MODERNITY. THE MADRID OF TODAY LEAVES NO-ONE INDIFFERENT. IT IS A PULSATING CITY OPEN TO THE WORLD IN WHICH IT HAS BEEN EASY TO ACCOMMODATE THE MOST CUTTING-EDGE SOCIAL AND CULTURAL MANIFESTATIONS. IT IS A MEETING POINT BETWEEN AMERICA, EUROPE AND AFRICA.

IN RECENT DECADES THE CITY HAS EXPERIENCED A SPECTACULAR URBAN TRANSFORMATION, ADAPTING ITS APPEARANCE TO THE NEW TIMES. IT HAS UNDERTAKEN CRUCIAL PROJECTS FOR RECOVERING THE RIVER MANZANARES OR FOR CREATING NEW GREEN SPACES. IT HAS ALSO MADE A BIG EFFORT IN IMPROVING ITS INFRASTRUCTURES AND CREATING OTHER NEW ONES. THE AIRPORT TERMINAL, THE SUCCESSIVE EXTENSIONS OF THE METRO NETWORK, THE HIGH-SPEED RAILWAY LINES OR THE PROJECT FOR THE NEW TECHNOLOGICAL PARK ARE ALL GOOD EXAMPLES OF THIS. MADRID HAS ALSO BECOME AN INTERNATIONAL REFERENCE POINT IN TERMS OF CONTEMPORARY ARCHITECTURE. SOME OF THE BEST ARCHITECTS IN THE WORLD ARE CARRYING OUT EMBLEMATIC PROJECTS FOR THE CITY. RAFAEL MONEO, JEAN NOUVEL, ÁLVARO SIZA, SANTIAGO CALATRAVA, SIR NORMAN FOSTER, ANTONIO LAMELA, RICHARD ROGERS OR THE HERZOG & DE MEURON STUDIO ARE PLACING MADRID AT THE HEAD OF WORLD ARCHITECTURE.

FORTUNATELY, ALL THESE NECESSARY TRANSFORMATIONS HAVE NOT CHANGED THE ESSENCE OF THE CITY. MADRID HAS TAKEN THE PATH TOWARDS MODERNITY, BUT HAS BEEN ABLE TO MAINTAIN THAT ESSENCE. IT IS STILL AN OPEN, WELCOMING, DIZZYING AND DISCONCERTING CITY THAT OPENS ITS ARMS TO WHOEVER VISITS IT.

Madrid Barajas Airport. Terminal T4.

P. 40

In recent years Madrid has achieved the difficult task of combining tradition with modernity. Projects such as the church of the convent of the Escuelas Pías de San Fernando represent this spirit to perfection. The new UNED library is integrated into the setting, respecting the remains of the old church.

P. 41

In the Lavapiés district there is a special symbiosis between old Madrid and the new cosmopolitan city. Here the traditional essence of the city coexists alongside the new airs that citizens from the five continents bring with them. This surprising and captivating mix cannot be ignored. The Plaza de Lavapiés is the epicentre of this delightful district with a maze-like layout. The majority of the buildings facing the square are from the 19th century. The recently opened Teatro Valle-Inclán, dependent on the Centro Dramático Nacional, introduces a touch of modernity to the space.

P. 42

The Planetarium, situated inside the Enrique Tierno Galván Park, is a source of knowledge regarding science and astronomy. Its main attraction is the spectacular multimedia projection room. Its location at around 60 metres height also makes it a marvellous viewpoint to look out over the city.

P. 43

As well as its overwhelming provision of museums, Madrid also has a large number of exhibition halls, foundations and cultural institutions which give space to the very latest artistic tendencies and latest social movements. Casa Encendida (in the photo), at number 2 Ronda de Valencia, stands out within this sphere due to its excellent installations and extensive cultural programme. Shortly opening in the Paseo del Prado will be CaixaForum, another centre of similar characteristics. Its main centre will occupy the rooms of the old Mediodía power station, the reform of which is being carried out by the prestigious Swiss architects Herzog & De Meuron.

P. 44, 45

Atocha Station is an excellent metaphor of the evolution of the city over the last 150 years. It was opened in 1851 and was Madrid's first-ever railway station. After being razed by a fire it was rebuilt in 1888 under the direction of Alberto Palacios, who was responsible for the lovely façade that faces the Emperador Carlos V roundabout. The last remodelling, undertaken between 1985 and 1992 by the architect Rafael Moneo, modernised the installations, quadrupling the station's capacity. The nave of the old station has been turned into a spectacular tropical garden with more than 500 different botanical species.

P. 46, 47

Madrid has had to adapt and improve its infrastructures notably in order to be able to meet the demands of constant demographic growth. One of the most interesting projects on these lines has been the rehabilitation of Príncipe Pío Station (the old Estación del Norte). After the reform undertaken between 1993 and 1994, the long-distance train section was replaced by a large interchange between metro transport, local trains and suburban bus lines. The beautiful original building was respected and inside a commercial centre has been built with a multi-screen cinema, shops and cafés and restaurants.

P. 48, 49

The construction of Gran Vía during
the first third of the last century sym-
bolised the emergence of a new
Madrid. The city began to look towards
the future and aspired to rival the other
grand European capitals. This lovely
avenue enabled the chaotic city centre
to be decongested. It immediately
became one of the symbols of the city.
Today it is still an essential thoroughfare, oriented towards leisure and with
a delightful cosmopolitan air.

P. 50, 51

Gran Vía ends at the busy Plaza de
España. The imposing monument to
Miguel de Cervantes overlooks this
open space. Around it stand out two
notable buildings constructed in the
middle of the last century by the
Otamendi brothers. The España building evokes the silhouette of North
American skyscrapers. Alongside it is
the Torre de Madrid, which at 130
metres in height was in its day the
tallest building in the city.

P. 52

The Plaza de Colón marks the end of Paseo de Recoletos and the beginning of Paseo de la Castellana. The presence of the Colón towers alerts the pedestrian to the fact that they are entering the financial heart of the city, an area dominated by contemporary architecture. These magnificent twin towers are noteworthy for their hanging structure and their characteristic deep red façade. They were built in 1976 by the architect Antonio Lamela. At their feet is the *Woman with Mirror*, one of the five sculptures by the Columbian Fernando Botero that can be seen spread around the streets of Madrid.

P. 53

Plaza de Colón. In 1977, in the gardens facing Calle de Serrano, the monument to the Discovery of America was installed, made by Joaquín Vaquero Turcios. They are three concrete macro-sculptures with inscriptions and relief work.

P. 54, 55

The famous *Hand* by Fernando Botero is situated in Paseo de la Castellana, where the Nuevos Ministerios buildings are. Very close to here is the Azca complex, one of the most important business centres in the city, its genuine Big Apple. Its twenty hectares of land house some of the most outstanding skyscrapers in Madrid, a point where the city shows its current drive to perfection.

P. 56

The BBVA building, with its characteristic ochre colour, result of the oxidation of the iron, is perhaps the most outstanding of the skyscrapers in the Azca complex. It was built by the architect Javier Sáenz de Oiza between 1979 and 1980.

P. 57

This beautiful tubular sculpture, work of José María Cruz Novillo, is situated at the foot of the spectacular Torre Picasso. The building was designed by the North American architect of Japanese origin Minoru Yamasaki, also author of the disappeared World Trade Center.

P. 58, 59

The two leaning towers that make up
what is called the Puerta de Europa,
popularly known as the Kio Towers,
have become since they were opened
(1996) one of the most representative
images of contemporary Madrid. They
are the work of the architects Philip
Johnson and John Burgee, and were the
first leaning skyscrapers to be built in
the world.

P. 60

The imminent conclusion of the Cuatro Torres Business Area will dramatically change the city skyline. The four buildings that make up the complex will easily surpass 200 metres in height. The Torre Repsol and the Torre de Cristal will become the ceiling of Madrid at 250 metres in height.

P. 61

With the construction of the new terminal (T4), the Madrid-Barajas airport has doubled its capacity, becoming one of the most modern and best-equipped in the world. This impressive infrastructure has been designed by the leading architects Antonio Lamela and Richard Rogers. The project has been awarded many international prizes for its magnificent construction. An exceptional entrance to a vibrant and contemporary city.

Living in Madrid

MADRID OVERFLOWS WITH LIFE. VISITING IT IS TO SUCCUMB TO THE CHARMS OF A BEAUTIFUL, CHAOTIC, FEVERISH, PASSIONATE, NOISY, SURPRISING CITY FULL OF CONTRASTS. WITH THE ARRIVAL OF DEMOCRACY AND THE LATER ENTRY INTO THE EUROPEAN UNION, THE CITY FINALLY SHOOK OFF ITS DARKEST AND MOST ISOLATIONIST PAST. IN JUST THREE DECADES IT HAS BECOME A LARGE, DYNAMIC AND CONTEMPORARY METROPOLIS. IN THIS BRIEF SPACE OF TIME IT HAS PLACED ITSELF AT THE ARCHITECTURAL, ECONOMIC AND CULTURAL VANGUARD, BUT WITHOUT LOSING SIGHT OF ITS HISTORY OR TURNING ITS BACK ON ITS PECULIAR WAY OF UNDERSTANDING LIFE.

THE PEOPLE OF MADRID ADORE THE STREET; YOU JUST NEED TO GO FOR A WALK AROUND THE CENTRE, AT ANY TIME OF DAY OR NIGHT, TO SEE FOR YOURSELF. WALKING ALONG ITS PACKED PAVEMENTS IT IS EASY TO BE SEDUCED BY ITS CONTAGIOUS VITALITY. THE CITY'S LEISURE OFFER IS EXTENSIVE: MUSEUMS WITH DESERVED WORLD FAME, NEW AND OLD-FASHIONED SHOPS, A MASSIVE CINEMA LISTING, BIG MUSICAL SHOWS, THEATRICAL PRODUCTIONS OF ALL KINDS, ACTIVITIES FOR CHILDREN, OPERA, DANCE, CONCERTS, EXHIBITIONS, CONFERENCES, MAGNIFICENT RESTAURANTS AND ITS FAMOUS NIGHTLIFE. A WIDE RANGE OF POSSIBILITIES CAPABLE OF SATISFYING ANY TASTE.

MADRID HAS ALWAYS BEEN A WELCOMING CITY. ITS MIXED IDENTITY HAS BEEN FORMED OVER THE CENTURIES WITH THE NUANCES THAT ATTRACTED PEOPLE FROM ALL THE CORNERS OF SPAIN. THE ARRIVAL IN RECENT YEARS OF PEOPLE FROM THE FIVE CONTINENTS OF THE WORLD HAS ENRICHED ITS CHARACTER EVEN MORE, FINALLY MAKING IT A MODERN AND COSMOPOLITAN LARGE CITY.

District of Las Letras

P. 64, 65

When a person from Madrid refers to the city centre, they are almost certainly thinking of the Puerta del Sol and the diffuse area that makes up the streets swirling around it. This popular square is the lively heart of the city, always busy at any hour of the day or night. From here leads to some of its most representative streets, such as Calle Mayor, Calle del Arenal (in the photo), Calle Preciados, Carrera de San Jerónimo or Calle de Alcalá. The Puerta del Sol is not perhaps the most beautiful spot in Madrid, but it is one of those that best defines its character and vitality. The moment of glory for this square takes place every 31st of December. This is when millions of Spanish people welcome in the New Year to the sound of the bells of the clock tower situated above the Real Casa de Correos, currently the offices of the Presidency of the Community of Madrid.

P. 66

The two most outstanding elements of the Puerta del Sol are the statue of the Bear and the Strawberry Tree, symbols of the city, situated facing Calle del Carmen; and the equestrian statue of Charles III, who has entered the history books as the best ever mayor of Madrid.

P. 67

The majority of the more traditional shops in the city are those bordering the Puerta del Sol and the Plaza Mayor. Strolling around this area, we come across hundred-year-old shops such as "La Favorita" hat and cap shop (in the photo) in Plaza Mayor; the famous "Casa Seseña" (Calle de la Cruz) specialising in capes; or the

many shops that sell military equipment and religious imagery. It is worth pointing out that there are also hundred-year-old cake shops, such as the old "El Pozo", senior member of the cake and pastry shops in Madrid; "Casa Mira" with its famous traditional *turrones* candies and marzipans; or the wonderful "El Riojano" cake shop.

P. 68

Any time is good for a beer or a glass of wine accompanied by a good tapa. A large part of the city's social life revolves around its infinite number of bars and restaurants. "Casa Labra" has been delighting its customers with its croquettes and its mythical cod slices since 1860.

P. 69

The well-lit advert for "Tío Pepe" sherry has overlooked the Puerta del Sol since the nineteen-thirties. It is the last survivor of the many advertisements that once crowned the square. This charming and unique image has become one of the most symbolic identifying marks of the whole city.

P. 70, 71

Some bars and restaurants form part of the living history of the city. The "Lhardy" restaurant, founded in 1839, has been able to conserve its delicious traditional atmosphere. This is also the case of "Casa Alberto", a traditional tavern whose delightful onyx and wood bar has been serving the public for more than 180 years.

P. 72, 73

There is nothing better than to shelter on a good terrace to chat, watch the world go by and combat the rigours of the Madrid summer. That of the Círculo de Bellas Artes, at number 42 Calle de Alcalá, is often frequented by personalities from the world of culture. The Círculo is one of the most classical and active cultural institutions in the city. Throughout the year it organises many exhibitions, conferences, book presentations, film cycles and theatrical performances. Its main centre is in a spectacular building which was the work of the architect Antonio Palacios in 1926.

P. 74, 75

The Plaza de Santa Ana, overlooked by the Teatro Español, is the heart of what is known as "el Barrio de Las Letras" the district of the arts. As well as for its beauty and undoubted interest that some of its buildings hold, this well known area is famous for its relaxing atmosphere and liveliness. Bohemian notoriety has always accompanied this delightful district. Some of the most famous figures of the history of Spanish literature have walked its streets and lived there. Here lived many of the great authors of the Golden Century: Geniuses of the category of Cervantes, Lope de Vega, Calderón, Tirso de Molina or Góngora.

P. 76

The archway of Cuchilleros is the most well-known gateway of the nine that lead to the Plaza Mayor. Its construction is a result of the reform undertaken by Juan de Villanueva after the fire that destroyed the square in 1790. It leads to the Cava de San Miguel, full of typical bars and restaurants.

P. 77, 78

El Rastro, which is held every Sunday and public holiday in the year, is without doubt the most popular street market in the city. In El Rastro you can find all kinds of goods, at all kinds of prices. It is a fascinating spot to walk around, shop and to soak up its incomparable atmosphere.

P. 79
The central Plaza de Tirso de Molina, with its recently-opened flower stalls, is one of the limits of El Rastro and of the working-class popular district of Lavapiés.

P. 80

In the Plaza de la Paja, of medieval origin, there is a delicious mix of the history of the city and its more entertaining and easygoing side. Here stand some important buildings, such as the Chapel of the Obispo, built between 1518 and 1535, with lots of terraces, bars and restaurants.

P. 81

The Plaza de San Andrés, alongside Plaza de la Paja, is the nerve centre of La Latina, one of the prettiest and more tourist districts of Madrid. The square features several buildings of great interest. The chapel of San Isidro (in the image), is a magnificent Baroque building constructed in the second half of the 17th century. Next to the chapel is the parish church of San Andrés and the interesting Museum of Origins. Both the square and the adjoining streets are full of life (particularly at the weekend) and are an excellent spot to have some tapas or enjoy the lively nightlife.

P. 82

Madrid possesses lots of cinemas. The Cine Doré, home of the Spanish Film Library, is surely the most beautiful of them all. This curious building with a Modernist air was built in the twenties. It is situated in the working-class district of Lavapiés, where in an indissoluble way what remains of the old Madrid is mixed with the more cosmopolitan and multicultural facet of the city.

P. 83

In an incomparable setting, between Atocha Station, the imposing building of the Ministry of Agriculture, the Botanical Gardens and the Parque del Retiro are in the pleasant Cuesta de Moyano. The 31 stalls that are placed here, where new and second-hand books are bought and sold, is an excellent place to spend the hours browsing amongst the many volumes on display to the pedestrian.

P. 84, 85

Gran Vía is the city's central avenue par excellence. Despite being a relatively recent thoroughfare, being built in the first half of the 20th century, it symbolises the pace and spirit of Madrid like few others. It is a street that is mainly dedicated to leisure, always busy at any time of day or night, where there are lots of fashion shops, cinemas and theatres, above all those showing the big musical shows. One of the essential ways of discovering the chaotic essence of the city and its people is to wander along the packed pavements of this lovely avenue.

P. 86

Madrid is a city for walking around. The distances between the different points of the centre can be easily covered on foot. Walking is the best way of fully taking in its peculiar idiosyncrasy, and there are lots of tree-lined avenues to be able to do it, such as the Paseo del Prado or the Paseo de Recoletos (in the image).

P. 87

The Plaza de Chueca is the centre of a district that has become really dynamic in recent decades. It has also become one of the centres of the gay community in the city. In its streets and squares many bars, discos, restaurants and shops of all kinds have sprung up oriented towards the gay consumer. It is a district with two distinct sides to it. At night it is one of liveliest and busiest areas of Madrid, whereas in the daytime it shows its more serene side, focused on small shops and the more day-to-day aspects of life.

P. 88

At number 239 Calle de Alcalá is the Las Ventas bullring, one of the most important bullrings in the world. It was designed by the architect José Espeliú in an attractive neo-Mudejar style. It is made in open brickwork over a metallic structure. It has a capacity for 25,000 spectators, mak-ing it the biggest in Spain. Inside is also the Bullfighting Museum that shows a large collection of items related to the world of bullfighting. The main bullfighting festival of the year is the Fair of Saint Isidoro, which begins in mid-May and lasts approxi-mately one month.

P. 89

At the "Marcial Lalanda" bullfighting school, in what is called the Venta del Batán (Casa de Campo), young hope-fuls prepare to become bullfighters one day in the future. While they practice the "muleta" movement they dream of being carried shoulder-high through the gates of Las Ventas.

Cultural Madrid

ALL CULTURE VULTURES ARE IN LUCK IN MADRID. THERE ARE FEW CITIES IN THE WORLD CAPABLE OF COMPETING WITH ITS CULTURAL RICHNESS AND WEALTH OF MUSEUMS. THE ENORMOUS AMOUNT OF ACTIVITIES THE CITY OFFERS COVERS ALL KINDS OF MATERIAL, STYLES AND PERIODS. IT INCLUDES SOME OF THE BEST ART COLLECTIONS IN THE WORLD AND A LARGE NUMBER OF SMALLER BUT EXTREMELY INTERESTING MUSEUMS. MANY OF THEM, DESPITE THEIR SINGULAR CHARM, GO UNJUSTLY UNNOTICED ON TOO MANY OCCASIONS.

THE THREE BIG MUSEUMS OF PASEO DEL PRADO DO NOT NEED INTRODUCING, MONOPOLISING THE ATTENTION OF LOCALS AND VISITORS ALIKE DUE TO THEIR UNDOUBTED INTEREST. BUT THE VAST CULTURAL SUPPLY OF THE CITY GOES WELL BEYOND THAT. DISTRIBUTED THROUGHOUT THE CITY THERE IS AN INFINITE NUMBER OF SMALL MUSEUMS AND CULTURAL INSTITUTIONS CAPABLE OF SATISFYING THE CONCERNS OF ALL KINDS OF AUDIENCE. CHILDREN WILL ENJOY THE RAILWAY, WAX AND FIREMEN'S MUSEUMS, OR IN THE FABULOUS COSMOCAIXA. CONTEMPORARY ART, ART BEING PRODUCED IN THE HERE AND NOW, HAS ITS SPACE IN THE NUMEROUS GALLERIES, EXHIBITION HALLS AND CULTURAL INSTITUTIONS OF THE CITY, IN CENTRES SUCH AS CASA ENCENDIDA, EL MATADERO, THE NEW CAIXAFORUM, OR THE MUNICIPAL MUSEUM OF CONTEMPORARY ART. THE MUSEUM OF AMERICA AND THE BLACK WORLD AFRICAN MUSEUM, AS WELL AS THE CASA DE AMÉRICA, THE CASA DE ASIA AND THE RECENTLY OPENED CASA ÁRABE WILL SATISFY ALL THOSE WHO WISH TO TAKE A LOOK AT OTHER CULTURES. AND OF COURSE THERE ARE THE NAVAL, AIR, DECORATIVE ARTS, BLIND AND NATURAL SCIENCE MUSEUMS TO MENTION JUST A FEW. ALL IN ALL, A VERY WIDE RANGE OF MUSEUMS AND ACTIVITIES WHICH, WITHOUT DOUBT, ARE WELL WORTH DISCOVERING.

Entrance doors to the extension of the Prado Museum produced by the sculptress Cristina Iglesias in bronze.

P. 92, 93

The Prado Museum has been, since it was opened in 1819, an absolute must to be visited by lovers of painting and art in general. This exceptional art collection is one of the best in the world and one of the great attractions of the city. Visiting it is to undertake a journey through the history of European painting. It is impossible to see it all in one day. Its exuberant collection ranges from 12th-century Romanesque murals through to the 19th-century. The Spanish school is extremely well represented and there are also great masterpieces of Italian, Flemish and, to a lesser extent, French and German painting. In the image, the Puerta de Murillo which opens before the Botanical Gardens.

P. 94

The Casón del Buen Retiro was the ballroom of the palace that Count-Duke de Olivares built for King Phillip Felipe IV in the 17th century. In 1971 the building, which had been used over time for different purposes, was handed over to the Prado Museum for its collection of 19th-century paintings to be hung. It is currently closed, undergoing rehabilitation work. In 2008 it will be opened as de Educational Centre of the Prado Museum.

P. 95

The building called Villanueva, in honour of Juan de Villanueva, architect of the project, was conceived in 1785 as a Natural History Museum. The work could not be completed until after the War of Independence (1808-1814). Its elegance makes it one of the unmistakable peaks of Spanish neoclassicism.

The statue of Diego de Velazquez overlooks the west façade, the main entrance to the museum. The brilliant Seville painter is magnificently represented inside with jewels of the category of *Las Meninas, The Spinners* or *The Surrender of Breda.*

P. 96, 97

The Reina Sofía National Museum Art Centre (MNCARS) is dedicated to contemporary artistic creation. Its collections range from the appearance of the vanguards in the 20th century through to art of today. The MNCARS collection includes the collections of the old Spanish Centre of Contemporary Art. The museum's most well-known work and its great attraction is undoubtedly Picasso's *Guernica*. As well as a good representation of the brilliant Malaga painter, its magnificent collection includes works by contemporary artists of the category of Dalí, Juan Gris, Joan Miró, Kandinsky, Bacon, Antonio Tàpies, Giacometti and Ibarrola, to mention just a few. Recently (2005) the new museum extension was opened, designed by the French architect Jean Nouvel.

On this page, one of the most representative images of the museum: the two transparent lifts that flank both sides of the main entrance. On the page on the right, the entrance to the museum extension.

P. 98

The Palacio de Cristal is in the Parque del Retiro, belongs to the Reina Sofía National Museum Art Centre (MNCARS) and includes installations produced for this building by artists from around the world. This beautiful building, almost completely made of iron and glass, was built in 1887 by the architect Ricardo Velázquez Bosco as a greenhouse for the General Exhibition of the Philippines.

P. 99

The spectacular triangle of art that is concentrated in Paseo del Prado is completed by the Thyssen-Bornemisza Museum. Its exceptional collection was acquired by the Spanish State from Baron Thyssen in 1993. The museum also houses in deposit the Carmen Thyssen-Bornemisza collection. There are a total of 1,000 works of art that cover the evolution of European painting from the 13th century until today. Worth mentioning is the representation of movements and styles such as German Renaissance, Impressionism, Expressionism, Russian Constructivism, Geometric Abstraction and Pop Art, making this museum complement its two illustrious neighbours to perfection.

P. 100, 101

In an imposing neoclassical building, on the side that leads to Calle de Serrano, is the National Archaeological Museum. Its collections trace the history of the Iberian Peninsula from prehistoric times to the 19th century. It also possesses important collections from Egypt and Greece, numismatics and a partial reproduction of a cave in Altamira. Its most well-known piece is *The Lady of Elche,* a peak of Iberian art. In the same building, on the side that leads to Paseo de Recoletos, is the National Library, whose archives include valuable manuscripts, incunabula, engravings, scores and photographs.

P. 102, 103

There are a large number of museums in Madrid that are often overshadowed by the three giants that stand on Paseo del Prado. The Lázaro Galdiano Museum, at number 122 Calle de Serrano, exhibits several paintings and items of decorative arts that belonged to private collection of the financier José Lázaro Galdiano (1862-1947). It is located in a small, early 20th-century palace that was his family home. Its excellent collection of paintings includes works by artists such as Francisco de Goya, El Greco, Bosch, Lucas Cranach, Mengs and Zurbarán. It also contains pieces of ivory, jewellery, furniture, embroidery and lacework, arms, medals and coins, ceramics and glasswork, drawings and engravings dating from the 7th to the 20th century.

P. 104

As well as big museums, there are many galleries, exhibition rooms and foundations in Madrid in which one can see the most contemporary art. The Fundación Juan March has been organising exhibitions, concerts and conferences since 1955. It is one of the most outstanding and active centres in the city

P. 105

The Museum of Public Art is perhaps the most surprising in the whole city. It is situated right in Paseo de la Castellana, under the raised walkway that joins Calle de Juan Bravo and Calle de Eduardo Dato. This curious location gives it an unmistakable urban and contemporary air. Its excellent collection is dedicated to abstract Spanish sculpture. It includes works by artists of the early vanguard movements, such as Joan Miró, Alberto and Julio González, and some of the most outstanding creative artists of the fifties generation, such as Jorge Oteiza, Pablo Palazuelo, Eduardo Chillida, Gerardo Rueda, Eusebio Sempere, Martín Chirino, Manuel Rivera, Gustavo Torner, José María Subirach, Audreu Alfaro, Rafael Leoz, Amadeo Gabino.

P. 106

The Sorolla Museum is in Calle del General Martínez Campos, very close to Paseo de la Castellana. It occupies a small early 20th-century palace and was the residence and studio of the Valencia painter. It conserves its original form and nearly all the rooms can be visited. Its collection includes, as well as many of Sorolla's works and personal objects, diverse pieces of sculpture, ceramics, furniture and popular jewellery.

P. 107

The imposing building of the old Barracas of Conde Duque is one of the great works that the architect Pedro de Ribera produced in Madrid. Today it houses the rooms of the Municipal Museum of Contemporary Art and three halls dedicated to temporary exhibitions. It is also the headquarters of the Municipal Newspaper Library, the City Archive and the Central Public Library. In summer the courtyard hosts part of the "Veranos de la Villa", summer in the city, programme of concerts.

P. 108

Another hidden jewel of the city is the Cerralbo Museum. Situated in a small 19th-century palace, residence of the Marquis of Cerralbo, it has a large and varied collection that includes European painting from the 16th to 19th centuries, sculptures, drawings, coins, decorative arts and diverse objects donated by the marquis after his death.

P. 109

In Calle de Fuencarral the building of the old Hospice of Madrid stands out, with its spectacular Baroque doorway. It was built by Pedro de Ribera between 1721 and 1726. Inside it houses the rooms of the History Museum (former Municipal Museum), which shows the historical and urban evolution of the city, the arts, the customs and the daily life of the people of Madrid from the 16th to the 20th century.

P. 110

A stone's throw from the Puerta del Sol, at the beginning of Calle Alcalá, is one of the great museums of Madrid, the Real Academia de Bellas Artes de San Fernando. Its magnificent painting collection includes three oil paintings by Goya, among which should be mentioned the famous *Burial of the Sardine*. Other great artists such as Zurbarán, Rubens, Mengs, Sorolla, Picasso or Juan Gris are also represented. It is also one of the few museums in the city that are open on Mondays.

P. 111

The Fundación Telefónica organises magnificent temporary exhibitions throughout the year. Its head office is in one of the most emblematic buildings in Gran Vía, the spectacular Telefónica building, which was the first American-style skyscraper in the city. This property also houses the rooms of the Telecommunications Museum.

P. 112

The small hermitage of San Antonio de la Florida, close to the Príncipe Pío Station, contains a marvellous surprise for art lovers. The building was erected with an elegant outline by the Italian architect Francisco Fontana between 1792 and 1798. However, what have undoubtedly given this temple world fame are the spectacular frescos with which Goya decorated its dome and pendentives. The hermitage was declared a National Monument in 1905. In 1919 the remains of the brilliant Aragon painter were moved to its interior.

P. 113

The Costume Museum, opened in 2004, provides a broad view of the evolution of clothing in Spain over the last five centuries. Its collection combines popular costumes from the different Spanish regions with items of hautecouture by designers such as Balenciaga, Pertegaz or Elio Berhanyer.

Madrid breathes

MADRID ALWAYS OFFERS AN OPPORTUNITY TO ESCAPE FROM THE HUSTLE AND BUSTLE OF THE FRENETIC PACE OF THE BIG CITY. ITS VAST NUMBER OF TREES (MORE THAN 250,000) AND ITS MORE THAN 250,000 HECTARES OF PARKS AND GARDENS SPREAD AROUND THE CITY, ENABLE THE PEOPLE OF MADRID AND VISITORS ALIKE TO EASILY ESCAPE FROM THE RIGOURS OF THE ASPHALT. IT IS THE GREEN MADRID, ONE OF THE MOST PLEASANT AND CHEERING SURPRISES THAT THIS BEAUTIFUL AND PASSIONATE CITY CONCEALS. IDEAL SPOTS TO STROLL, RELAX AND ENJOY THE PLANTLIFE.

THE PARQUE DEL RETIRO IS, IN ITS OWN RIGHT, THE MOST FAMOUS AND MOST-VISITED IN THE CITY. ITS GREAT SCENIC AND MONUMENTAL RICHNESS, ITS LOCATION IN THE VERY HEART OF THE CITY, ITS PECULIAR IDENTITY AND THE GREAT VARIETY OF ACTIVITIES IT PLAYS HOST TO, MAKE EL RETIRO IMMEDIATELY SEDUCE EVERYONE WHO VISITS IT.

THE QUANTITY AND DIVERSITY OF GREEN AREAS THAT THE CITY POSSESSES IS IMPRESSIVE. PALATIAL GARDENS, SUCH AS THE SABATINI GARDENS OR CAMPO DEL MORO; ENGLISH-STYLE PARKS SUCH AS THE SPECTACULAR PARQUE DEL OESTE; AUTHENTIC LIVING MUSEUMS, SUCH AS THE DELICIOUS BOTANICAL GARDENS, WITH MORE THAN 30,000 PLANT SPECIES FROM ALL OVER THE WORLD; LESS CROWDED SPOTS WITH A SINGULAR CHARM, SUCH AS QUINTA DE LOS MOLINOS OR THE FUENTE DEL BERRO; CORNERS FULL OF MAGIC AND ROMANTICISM SUCH AS THE EL CAPRICHO PARK, IN THE ALAMEDA DE OSUNA; OR RECENTLY CREATED PARKS, SUCH AS THE JUAN CARLOS I PARK AND THE MANZANARES PARK. A WIDE RANGE OF BEAUTIFUL, QUIET AND SUGGESTIVE SPACES.

Entrance to the Parque del Retiro by Calle de Alfonso XII.

P. 116, 117

The Parque del Retiro is the green space par excellence of Madrid. Its great beauty and privileged location in the city centre are an irresistible attraction for everyone who is looking for a few moments of peace and the pleasant refuge of the vegetation. Conceived originally in the 17th century as a recreational property for the monarchy, today it has become a delicious meeting point open to everyone. It is a park full of life, ideal for taking part in any of the many activities held there or simply to sit down and watch the world go by: an oasis of peace and fresh air in the middle of the asphalt.

P. 118, 119

The lake is one of the most famous identifying images of the Parque del Retiro. The image of the boats gliding across the water, with the spectacular monument to Alfonso XII as a backdrop, has become a symbol of both the park and the city of Madrid. The imposing monument, made in bronze and marble, consists of a beautiful colonnade arranged around the equestrian statue of the king and a stairway that drops to the water, adorned with stone lions and bronze allegories. It was built by the architect José Grasses Riera in 1902.

P. 120

The "Bosque del Recuerdo" (Wood of Memory) pays homage to the 191 victims who lost their lives in the brutal bombings on the 11th of March 2004 in Madrid and to the officer killed in the later police operation. It consists of 192 trees (22 olive trees and 170 cypresses), one for each of the victims.

P. 121

The statue of the Fallen Angel stands out among the monumental richness of the Parque del Retiro for its beauty and originality. It is one of the few statues dedicated to the devil in the world. It is in the Paseo del duque Fernán Núñez, on the site that was once occupied by the old Fábrica de Porcelanas de la China. It was produced by the sculptor Ricardo Bellver in 1874. It represents Lucifer expelled from Paradise with a snake coiled around him. The statue won prizes for its quality and fine production at the National Exhibition of Sculpture of 1878. It has occupied its current site since 1885.

P. 122, 123

The Palacio de Cristal, situated on the shore of a small lake, is possibly the most important building in the Retiro. It was built in 1887 by the architect Ricardo Velázquez Bosco as a greenhouse for exotic plants for the General Exhibition of the Philippines. It is made almost entirely of iron and glass, following the design of the Crystal Palace of London. Today, just like the Palacio de Velázquez, another building by the same author also located in the park, it depends on the Reina Sofía National Museum Art Centre and regularly houses temporary exhibitions of contemporary art.

P. 124, 125

The Royal Botanical Gardens are the perfect spot for taking a break along the route and enjoying some nature. The richness of its vegetation and its unique charm make it one of the most interesting green spaces in Madrid. It is situated in Paseo del Prado, in the cultural heart of the city. Its construction between 1774 and 1781 formed part of the enlightened measured adopted by the monarch Charles III. Two of the best architects of the time, Francisco Sabatini and Juan de Villanueva, were entrusted with the project. The garden is arranged in three staggered terraces and also has a magnificent green-house dedicated to species from desert, tropical and sub-tropical species. It possesses a total of more than 30,000 plant species from the five continents of the world. It also has an exhibition room, a magnificent herbarium, a library and an important historical archive. It is a genuine museum of nature and a delight for the senses.

P. 126, 127

Casa de Campo is a large forested area to the west of the city. Its more than 1,700 hectares make it one of the big breathing spaces of Madrid. Its origins, given its closeness to the Palacio Real, were closely linked to the crown. Phillip II acquired the land in order to have a large game reserve close to his residency. Casa de Campo continued belonging to the monarchy for several centuries. Only after the arrival of the Second Republic did it pass into municipal hands and open to the public. Today it is a leisure-oriented green space that is very popular among Madrid's locals. The wood is home to many species of trees, such as pines, poplars, chestnuts, black poplars, holm oaks, planes, ashes, oaks and willows.

P. 128, 129

Casa de Campo, as well as the peace and quiet of its natural setting, has many leisure options for visitors. It has sports facilities, bars and restaurants, a lake, zoo, amusement park and several trade fair precincts. This makes it one of the favourite leisure spots for Madrid families. Perhaps the most exciting way of approaching it is the cable car that links it with the nearby Parque del Oeste, one of the most beautiful in Madrid. The route is 2.5 km long and reaches a total height of 40 m. From this privileged perspective one can get spectacular views of the city and its environs.

P. 130

The Parque del Oeste stands out for its English-style layout and its steep slopes. It was designed at the beginning of the last century by the architect Cecilio Rodríguez and occupies a space measuring 98 hectares. Strolling along its paths reveals some marvellous corners. One of the most interesting is La Rosaleda where an International Competition of New Roses is held every May: it is located in the lower part of the park.

P. 131–133

The Temple of Debod is the oldest monument in Madrid and one of the most surprising. Its origin dates back to the 2nd century BC. It was a gift from the Egyptian government to the Spanish one in 1970. It was originally sited in Lower Nubia and it was moved to make way for the Aswan Dam. It is an excellent spot for taking in the famous Madrid sunsets.

P. 134, 135

The Parque del Manzanares is in the south of the city, between the river and the M-30 road, and covers more than 500 hectares. It forms part of the ambitious recovery project of the banks of the river undertaken by the local authorities. It is one of the most important green area developments that the city possesses. The sculpture known as *The Lady of Manzanares* crowns the watchtower situated in the park, and is the work of the Valencia artist Manolo Valdés. It is made in bronze and steel, weighs eight tons, is 13 metres high and has a spectacular illumination system. From the top of the watchtower there is a wonderful view of Madrid, and on clear days one can even make out the Guadarrama mountain range.

P. 136, 137

The Parque Juan Carlos I is one of the most modern in Madrid. It is in the northeast of the city, in Campo de las Naciones, next to the trade fair centre, in an area close to Barajas airport. It was opened in 1992, measures 160 hectares and is possibly the most contemporarily-designed park in the city. A great many activities are organised in the park: skating, angling, kite flying, remote controlled boats, etc. It also has long pathways, sports facilities and a free bicycle hire service to tour its nine-kilometre circuit. Another of its attractions are the 19 large-scale sculptures that adorn it (in the photo one can see the work *Dedos* (Fingers) by the Chilean sculptor Mario Irarrázabal). In summer, in what is called the "cybernetic fountain", there are splendid shows of light, water and sound.

P. 138, 139

El Capricho, one of the most beautiful and romantic parks in the city, is situated in the Alameda de Osuna. It was built at the behest of María Josefa Alonso Pimentel, Duchess of Osuna, the famous patron of Francisco de Goya and great lover of the art world. The French Jean Baptiste Mulot and the Spanish López Aguado were entrusted to express the duchess's desires. A sinuous stream, the lake, the jetty, the labyrinth of bushes, the different fountains or the shrine of Baco (in the photo) make up this authentic jewel that lets the imagination fly.

P. 140, 141

At number 500 Calle de Alcalá, in the San Blas district, far away from hustle and bustle of the city centre, is one of the least known, beautiful and surprising green spaces in the city, the Parque de la Quinta de los Molinos. It is an old agricultural property, with a rural air, where there are lots of flowers and trees, mainly almond and olive trees, but also cypresses, pines and eucalyptuses. It is a lovely spot, particularly in spring, when one can see the spectacle of the blossoming almond trees. The estate belonged to the Count of Torres-Arias and later the architect César Cort, who in the 1920s built the small palace being rehabilitated to house the Fundación Magistralia, dedicated to teaching music.

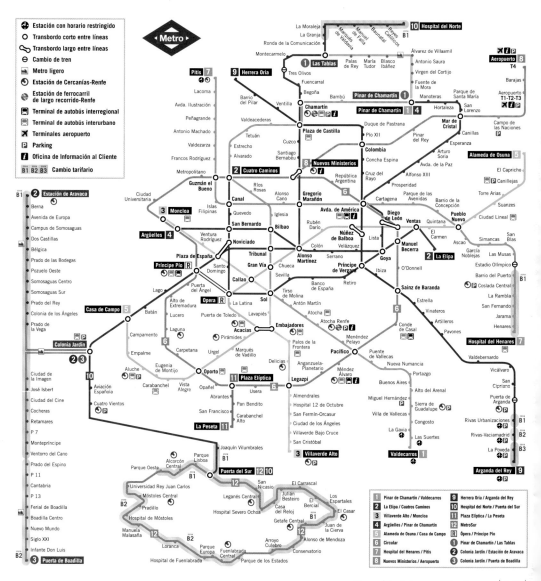

We would like to thank all the entities and individuals that have made it possible to publish this book through their collaboration.

Published by: Ediciones Aldeasa
Editorial Coordination: Carmen de Francisco

Text: Pablo Caballero
Translation from Spanish: Steve Cedar
Photography: All the photographs in this book have been taken out from Archivo Ediciones Aldeasa, except those detailed below: Daniel Bellido, 73, 85; David Jiménez, 38, 61; Hidalgo-Lopesino, 8-9, 16-17, 41, 42, 43, 44, 45, 46, 47, 48-49, 60, 66, 67, 70, 75, 80, 102-103, 104, 106, 109, 110, 124, 125, 128, 134, 135, 139.
Cover photograph: Archivo Ediciones Aldeasa

Design and layout: Estudio OdZ
Cartography: Paul Coulbois
Subwaymap: Pedro Monzo
Typeset: Cromotex
Printed by: Brizzolis

© of this edition: Ediciones Aldeasa, 2008
© of the photography: Archivo Ediciones Aldeasa
ISBN: 978-84-8003-783-9
Legal Registration nº: M-44-544-2007
Printed in Spain